MACKENZIE THORPE

FROM THE HEART

MACKENZIE THORPE

FROM THE HEART

SIMON & SCHUSTER
A VIACOM COMPANY

Cover picture: The Last Temptation
Front endpaper: Boys' Heads–Class
Back endpaper: Girls' Heads–Class
Half title: The Drip
Title: Forward
Contents: Cuckoo in the Nest
This page: The Horizon

First published in Great Britain by ibooks, 2000
Simon & Schuster UK Ltd
A Viacom Company

00 01 02 03/10 9 8 7 6 5 4 3 2 1

Designed by Guy Callaby and Michael Haines
for Threefold Limited, London

Edited by Dinah Dunn

Printed in England

An ibooks, inc. Book

Simon & Schuster UK Ltd.
Africa House
64-78 Kingsway
London WC2 6AH

Simon & Schuster Australia
Sydney

A CIP catalogue record for this book is available from the
British Library

ISBN 0-7434-1324-5

This book is about the truth,
a truth for so many.
A truth that shows the color
and hope within life's struggles.

Mackenzie Thorpe 2000

I am the eldest child of seven, born in a three-bedroom council house in the center of Middlesbrough, an industrial town in northern England. I remember so much from those days: the fun and laughter, the sounds, the struggles, the personalities. I remember it all.

There was little luxury. Three pennies a week would be my pocket money, if I got any. I would spend my time drawing, keeping out of trouble by retreating into my own little world. With no extra money for paper, I'd unwrap cigarette packets, flatten them, and draw on them. Nothing deterred me. I would draw on anything, anywhere I could.

I left school at fifteen. I didn't get any qualifications because of my dyslexia and so I did what everyone else did: I got a job at the local shipyards. It was manual, unskilled work but it felt good to take home a wage. I met great men, proud and hardworking. In that harsh, unforgiving environment I shared their laughter and witnessed their pain. I saw the men fighting each other deep in the bowels of huge ships, tired men struggling to get through their day, waiting for the sound of the siren to set them free, and I saw it all through the eyes of a boy in a big man's world. I knew I couldn't live out my life there.

I was still drawing, but getting more and more frustrated. My close friend Adrian, who was wiser and more knowledgeable than me, suggested I go to art school. In my world it was almost ridiculous—no one I knew had ever been to any kind of college. My application form was terrible, with spelling mistakes galore, and it was clear enough that I couldn't write essays. But I had literally hundreds of drawings. The college recognized the level of my commitment and, on the strength of my work, accepted me. I was in!

After a few years I transferred from the local art college to the Byam Shaw School in London. For the first time in my life I had access to paintings in major galleries, which changed my whole way of thinking, as well as the direction of my art. From then on I just ate and drank modern art. Rothko, especially, remains one of my inspirations. I realized from the work that I studied how important it was to put myself, Mackenzie Thorpe, into my paintings.

Introduction

This book you are holding will show you a selection of my work. I'm proud and honored to have my work viewed by such a large audience. I always paint the truth; I am not an illustrator. For me the image is the vehicle to encourage and enable people to feel and think about their emotions. A canvas, a piece of paper, or a subject can be approached by the artist on many different levels.

My work does not have to be totally representative. Somebody looking at a photo of my son would see two eyes, a nose, a mouth—just a picture of his outer surface. I am not trying to re-create this outer image. I want to show his character, his beauty, his innocence. That is what I am always striving to create—the emotion, the feeling. If I have been successful in my work, when people view it, they will tap into their own hearts and souls, giving the work their own emotional interpretation. That's why I leave out many of the details in my work—details can be obstacles to looking beyond the surface. I love looking beyond and I want others to look beyond with me. When I paint something, I want everybody to relate to it—wherever they are from and whatever their background. They don't have to read it because they feel it. Say it's an image of a big smiley giraffe poking his head above the flowers. There's nothing threatening there. It's totally soft and gentle, full of blue sky and bright sunshine, with this wacky giraffe, laughing his head off. You laugh with it and you see the innocence and the humor and the tenderness. People from all nationalities or ages understand what's going on in that picture. They all see it and it stirs their emotions.

I paint with all of my passion, with everything I've got. That's why it works, because I don't hold back. I draw and paint because I have to. If people stopped looking at my work, I would still draw. Of course it is wonderful that people do enjoy my work, but I drew before success came and whatever happens in my life, I know I will draw and paint until I die.

This book is an introduction to my work and a way of showing people through my experiences that there are so many things worth living for—so much joy, so much hope. Sometimes we have to look a bit harder to find it, but it is always worth it. My work says, "Live with a passion and thoughtfulness for others and yourself. Celebrate life. Be aware of what you're doing and your world can be a good place."

At the End of the Day

When I first set up the Art Haus shop in North Yorkshire, money didn't come easily. My work was still developing and was not widely understood. That's when I did the first square sheep. I didn't think about what I was doing when I painted it. I just drew this shape and then put a head and legs on it and it became my self-portrait, standing solid, facing the world for all to see.

I had studied art therapy, so I knew that the canvas, no matter what its size, is the universe and whatever art is placed on it is within that universe. If you look at my world on the canvas, you've got this big square shape and it's a self-portrait. So I was filling that universe with me, standing tall, with four legs on the ground, the landscape behind me, and my head touching the sky.

I understood later why the sheep was square. It represented society's narrow-mindedness and rejection of things new or different. But after I had a near-fatal car accident, the sheep came to mean something different to me, more to do with my wife and kids. My family is one of the biggest influences on me now, I love them with all of my heart. I'll draw a picture and it'll be so bright, I'll like it so much that I'll call it "Owen" or "Chloe" or "Susan," because I want them to have it, it's for them. It's about the love and closeness we are so privileged to share.

Painting the square sheep was a way of empowering myself, like putting feelings down on paper so they could reflect back to me. You would think that when I'm working on pictures of big smiley faces, I must be really happy. Sometimes it's the other way around. It allows me to move on in times of depression or anger. When I work in that way my mood lifts and I start having a ball—putting the piece of paper up, turning on some loud, inspiring music, then drawing a big smiley face. I change the focus of my mood. I wasn't aware of it until my wife Susan pointed it out. It's a way of saying you can be happy if you choose to be.

Love and Family

In the Woods

ANIMALS I don't see the point in painting a portrait—you might as well take a photograph. But to paint someone's personality, what's beneath the surface, is much more meaningful. So, I'll paint someone as a big smiley giraffe or a horse with its mane blowing in the wind to show the different sides of their personality.

Cock-a-Doodle-Doo

Overleaf
Love His Mane   Lawrence II   Endless Love

A Bleating Heart

In the Heart of Winter

SUNFLOWERS

Sunflowers are a tribute
to Van Gogh. When I
first saw *Lust for Life*, the
film about Van Gogh's
life and work, I realized
that I had the same
drive to paint, no matter
what the odds. I
understood that I wasn't
here to work in the
shipyards, but that my
purpose was to paint the
truth in my life.

The Sunshine of My Life

From the **moon**
The **eyes**
Of her **soul**
From the **hands**
Through my **heart**

Susan

Susan

Chloe

Owen

OWEN AND CHLOE Sometimes I wake up in the morning and feel a bit down. I will go into the kitchen and Chloe will be there, my lovely fourteen year old, talking and laughing, gossiping like all teenage girls do, moaning about her hair or school or whatever. I can always get a hug from her and feel so privileged. Owen is sixteen, taller than me now. I'm so proud of him. He is so much fun. He doesn't fight or steal or get into trouble—he's just a nice guy. Whenever I feel the slightest bit down, I only have to think about these two, look out of the window and think how good it all is.

In the Land of Love

Pig in Snow

Taking the Dog Out

Front and Side Elevation

Dog with a Family

Leading the Bull

Bringing the Water

Underburden

Before the Wind Blows

A Little Further Down the Road

SHEPHERDS I'm a man who is able to wash his own clothes. I do ironing, I cook and clean and I go to work. I don't have any problems with this. I do these things because I want clean clothes and we need to eat and these are not difficult tasks. I expect to share the workload, I want to be a good and fair person, and I don't have to live by other people's rules of what a man should and should not do.

The shepherd in my work is that all-around person—not just a man, but a person. This shepherd will walk through the wilderness; he will stand atop the highest mountains; he will go without food and shelter to look after his flock. I want to be a man who will look after a child, care for his flock, protect them, love, guide, and nurture them. I will do whatever it takes to keep them safe and happy.

I Saw the Light

Reach Out and Touch

With all my heart
and passion...

...no

matter

what,

we

will

come

through.

Getting There

I was born in my grandmother's living room in the heart of Middlesbrough, by the majestic transporter bridge. Eleven of us lived there, all crowded together. Inside of that house I was safe, eating grandma's apple pie, sitting on grandad's knee. Outside I was vulnerable. I didn't fit in either at school or on the street. Reading and writing seemed impossible for me to master. I was not a good fighter, nor a streetwise little toughie. My uncle Lawrence, who was three years older, protected me. He held himself well in that environment, he spoke the right language, the language of the streets. I could only draw and that set me apart even further. I got picked on, I got shouted at, I got humiliated, I got knocked down. I guess I retreated into myself as a means of protection, to stop the rejection and isolation I felt from hurting too much.

It was twenty years before my wife, Susan, came into my life and for the first time I felt it was safe to show my love, passion, and joy, freely and openly. A lot of my paintings of children are saying, "Just give me a chance. Don't step over me, don't disregard me, don't hurt me. Love and respect me."

When We Were Young

BEES The first time I drew a bee, I wanted to put a little "bzzzz" into the picture because sound is a part of life. I started to employ it more and more. But then I got stung on the arm by a bee and it swelled so big I couldn't bend it. If I had been in the wilderness and was stung on my throat or my head, would I have died, my airways swollen, gasping for breath? This tiny little bee could have been my downfall. I feel it was a reminder not to overlook things in life.

Self with Bees

Collecting the Red

CHILDREN WITH FLOWERS Children are
the source of love—they plant it at our feet,
nurture it, and help it grow throughout our lives.

Avalon

Love and Joy

BIG HEADS The idea is that we are all born the same, equal. As we grow, we impose restrictions on ourselves and on our children. We are not born afraid of the dark. We are not born racists. We are not born frightened of spiders. We learn to be scared of new adventures, of new foods, of new experiences, and so our world shrinks. This fear is all between our ears—it's not real. Yet we persist in living it and passing it on instead of welcoming and sharing the joy of the new and the unknown. For me, the big heads symbolize children: new, uncorrupted, their heads full of endless possibility, open to whatever comes their way. It is only as we grow older that we become narrow and closed. Let's keep our heads as big as possible. Continue to marvel at the beauty of nature, revel in the smell of the flowers, and thank God you're alive.

Mother Winter

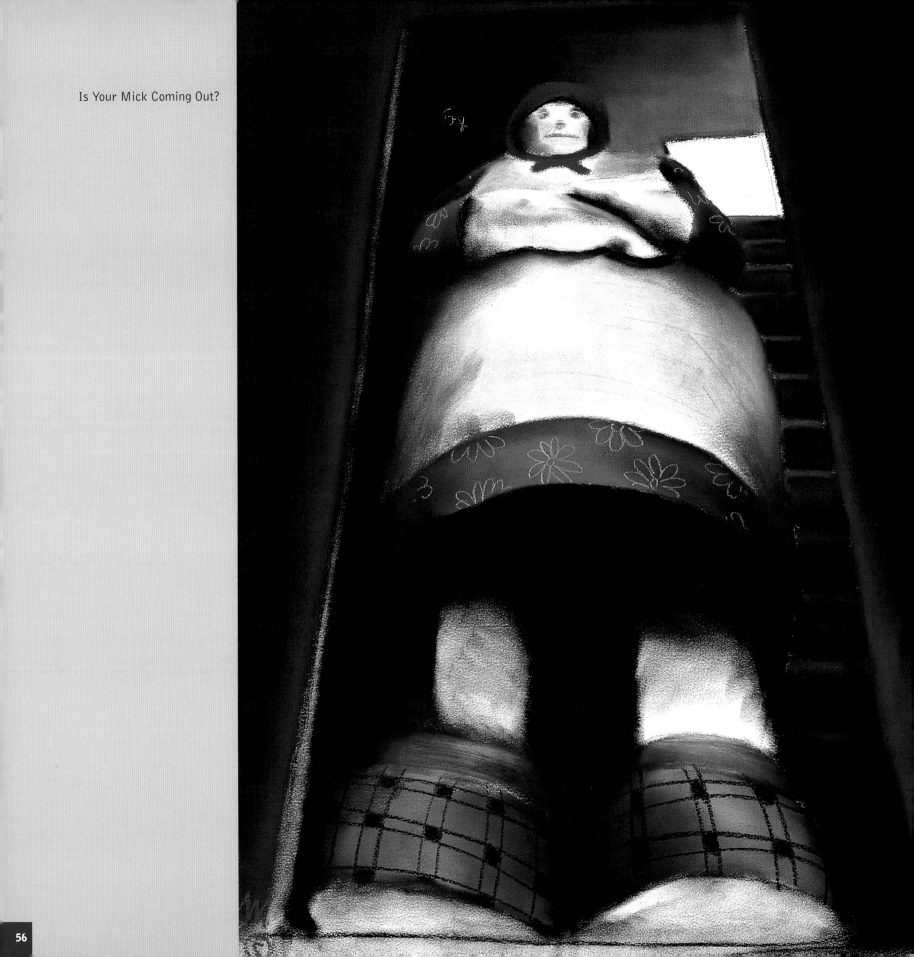

She filled the door
The house, the world

Home of the Brave

FISH IN A GLASS JAR The fragility of the soul is like a fish in a glass jar. You must protect it at all times and know that once your soul is out of the jar it is vulnerable to the dangers of the world.

Flying a Kite

First Day in a New World

Sitting with Grandad

Family

Never Out of Danger

CHILDREN IN DUFFLE COATS Sometimes when I paint a child, he might not have a face. Without a face, he's every child. The cloth of his coat is hardy and plain, his shoes sturdy. Sometimes he has so little, I paint him without a shadow. The landscape is barren, without flowers or trees. The child is totally alone.

But then I might add a bit of color, trying to put some hope in the picture. Because you know that if you invited this child inside, gave him a bath, cooked him dinner, and shared some time with him, it wouldn't be long before you saw the real person within. The child would smile, play games, and talk to you. He'd trust you after a while, his defenses would crumble, and you would see his love and compassion.

Rider of Love

High on a Lonely, Windy Hill

Six penn'orth with vinegar, salt and scraps on…

Iveno

And I shall
Walk the walk
With truth
In my hand

Middlesborough Baddies

When We Were Young

Tomorrow never came
We lived in our dreams

A Parkend Cowboy

El Gringo

The Outlaw

Jake

The Outlaw

Summer 1965

On Top of the World

My hometown of Middlesbrough, England, comes through a lot in my work. I'm so proud of it. An outsider might find it hard to be proud of shipyards and steelworks, but I am. I know what's behind that outer layer. When you know these people, when you grow up with them, this is your world. They're your brothers, your fathers, your grandfathers. When I was a child I would see my Grandad going out to work in the morning, and coming home in the evening, tired and dirty, and I would sense his pride. Early in the morning I would hear the sounds of the baker delivering bread, the van's tires on cobbled streets, the greetings exchanged: "Morning George." Late in the evenings, I could hear the sounds of men singing in the distance, sometimes arguing, their bellies full of ale, opinions strengthened by the effects.

I draw and paint the streets of my hometown, but they really could be anyone's. We all have our memories, those warm nostalgic feelings that wash over us, when we remember with fondness.

Heading Home

Left for Dead

WORKING MAN With some of my paintings, I'm building a monument to the working men who no longer have jobs. The ships aren't built in my town anymore; the steel and iron have gone. The men are now unemployed. I'm putting that precious history down on canvas.

I want to capture the passion of when they did work: the molting of the metal, the sound of hammers on steel. There was a pride, a beauty in these men. Their lives were hard, but they worked even harder and were valued and had a sense of purpose. Now some of these proud strong men have not had a job for twenty years or more. Their heads hang down, they don't use their strength, their arms. In some of my work you will see their arms are gone, unneeded.

It's tragic and cruel— these men want to work but the jobs are no longer there for them.

Towards Home

On His Way

Middlesborough Stand Off

Time

Hell Frozen

Building a Ship

Nearly There   A Kiss to See Me Through

Heading Home

Toward Me

Shoppers

Overleaf
It Was Shrouded in Darkness

For me, love is the most important thing. Nothing else comes close. All of the riches in the world cannot compare to the love I share with my family. Sometimes I will draw children surrounded by flowers, smiling and happy. These images are symbols of the sheer joy and love of life, for the innocence and beauty and hope I see all around me. It is a source of strength and pride to me and it's there for us all.

Like a delicate flower, love can be easily crushed through purpose or neglect. Yet still, in the hottest desert or the highest mountain, a flower will find a way to grow. No matter how you cover a seed, the flower will find a way to survive. You can't stop it from growing. And if you put it in a nice pot with sunshine and water, you'll end up with a bush which will grow and blossom, leading to many flowers.

The Loved

Taking Them Out

Of a smile

Self with John

BIG FEET The big feet symbolize that I never want to forget where I came from, no matter how different my life has become. It can be dangerous to forget your roots. Your ego takes over, and you've got wings on your feet. If I got too full of myself, I wouldn't be the man Susan fell in love with and married. I wouldn't be the father of my children. My feet are firmly planted on the ground, and that's where I want them to stay, totally grounded. It's important never to become bigger than your shoes.

The Lovers

The Searchers

Flowers for Christmas

And through the snow

he brings you

his

Love

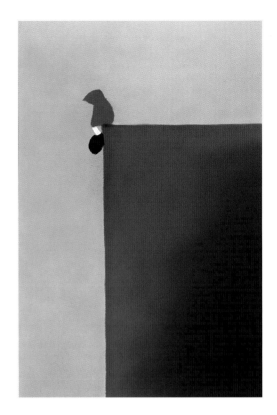

Sitting

CLIFFS There have been many transitions in my life, like when I decided to pursue my career as an artist. My family comes with me to the edge of these new experiences and together we look over "the cliff" and know that everything will be just fine.

The Ecstasy

The Visit

Lost and Found

Return to Me

I try to bring hope with my art. We all have hopes and dreams, which we should hold on to, because they tell us what we really want in life. No matter how big, how wild, how outrageous our dreams are, they can point us in the direction that is going to give us fulfillment and happiness. Everyone—from lawyers to laborers—faces life's challenges. Most people have gone through some form of hardship and some have grown as a result. In all of hardship there is a glimmer of light; it may be very small, but it's there. I want people to laugh and I also want them to know it's okay to cry. By remembering our struggles we can see just how far we have traveled.

Sometimes my life has been a dark tunnel, but a productive dark tunnel. You've got to do your best to come out at the other end. All sorts of things have happened in my life, but I'm here, I've survived. I have hope and joy and it's there in my work.

Hope

Don't use words
Nor eyes
Feel

Gloria

The Bud

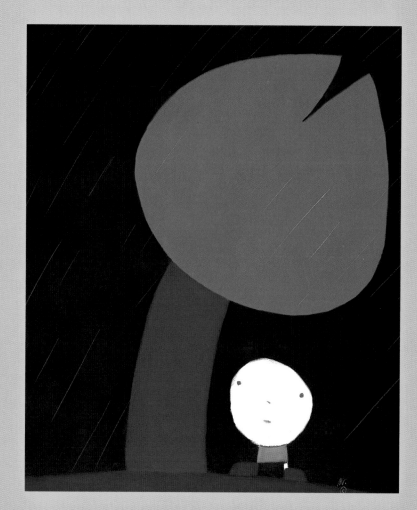

Sheltering

Don't Let Them Down

For some
Hardship ...
But he has
The Beauty

Previous page
Rattle and Hum

Flying Away

Chasing a Cloud

BRIDGES Certain symbols continue to reappear in my work. I work on and around them for a time and then move on, only to return to them on some later date.

In my earlier work you rarely see bridges—I just didn't draw them. Then suddenly they were there, in industrial scenes with chimney stacks and smoke. Maybe the bridge symbolizes finding ways around the obstacles, over the obstacles, getting into new environments, meeting new challenges. Or maybe just moving forward, going from one place to the next. I think that's part of what I'm doing in my life.

Man Walking

I can
Live
Forever
In your
Trust
Of hope

Holding on to Life

Soon Home

In this world
Of despair
There is an
Overwhelming   Man By Pain
Abundance
of Hope

CLOUDS Every cloud is a struggle, every ripple a hardship. But at the same time there is always light breaking through. In life you need to experience both sides of this sky to gain appreciation for the light.

Crossing the Sea

Previous page
Leaving Gamora . . . to the Promised Land

Mackenzie Thorpe, born 1956   Middlesbrough, North Yorkshire

EDUCATION

Middlesbrough College of Art   Middlesbrough, North Yorkshire
Byam Shaw School of Art   London

ONE-MAN SHOWS

The Last Chance Centre	London 1984
The 181 Gallery	London 1986
The Escape Gallery	London 1990
St. Martin-in-the-Fields	London 1991, 1992
Kings Head Hotel	Richmond, Yorkshire 1993
The Glass House Gallery	Yorkshire 1993
The Halcyon Gallery, Selfridges	London 1994
The Phoenix Gallery, Selfridges	London 1995
Halcyon Gallery	Birmingham, England 1995
Allerton Castle	Knaresborough, Yorkshire 1995
The Soan Gallery	London 1995
Ozten Zeki Gallery	London 1996
Halcyon Gallery	Birmingham, England 1996
Art Connoisseur Gallery	London 1996
Hexton Gallery	New York 1997
Halcyon Gallery	Birmingham, England 1998
Hanson Gallery	Sausalito, California 1997, 1998, 1999
R. Roberts Gallery	Jacksonville, Florida 1998
Hanson Gallery	New Orleans, Louisiana 1998
Images Fine Art	Napa Valley, California 1998
Hanson Gallery	Carmel, California 1998, 1999
Kenneth Behm Galleries	Seattle, Washington 1998
Atlas Galleries	Chicago, Illinois 1999

JOINT EXHIBITIONS

The Tom Allen Centre	London 1985
West Ham Town Hall	London 1986
The Ginger Gallery	Bristol 1990
The Laguna Art Festival	Laguna Beach, California 1991
The Highgate Gallery	London 1992
The Blackheath Gallery	London 1992, 1993
Artexpo Los Angeles	Los Angeles 1996
Tressors Art Fair	Singapore 1997
Artexpo New York	New York 1997, 1998, 1999
CMF Gallery	New York 1999

SPECIAL COMMISSIONS AND HONORS

1995
Allerton Castle Exhibition. Largest one-man show
ever held at this 19th-century landmark.

1995
Commissioned to create a series of hand-pulled serigraphs
for European market.

1996
Artexpo Los Angeles. Selected as lead artist
for show poster and catalog cover.

1996
Commissioned to create second series of hand-pulled serigraphs
for international market.

1996
Elton John AIDS Foundation Commission. Holiday card design.

1997
Presentation to Her Royal Highness, Princess Anne.
Contributed painting to HRH's Save the Children Fund.

1997
British Dyslexia Foundation Holiday card design.

1998, 1999, 2000
William Hague, British Conservative Party Leader.
Holiday card design.

Shows

Tom

Index

Happy Landing

COLOR Let's say a child does a pencil drawing, an outline, and it's brilliant. But when she puts color in it—a green sky and purple trees—the teacher says it's wrong and the drawing is ruined. That's when she learns to be frightened of color. I draw and create shapes using color. And that allows me to dive in the deep end and explore, like the same way a three year old does in kindergarten. Bish, bosh, bash, and it's finished. "What is it?" you ask. And she says, "Oh that's my house and that's dad coming home from work and there's the dog and my swing in the garden." Her whole world is there, in those colors. And the sad thing is, when children get older, they don't paint like that anymore. I'm trying to use color to get back to that place, where I can draw with feeling and emotion, where it is impossible to make mistakes.